Big Machines At Work

Street Cleaners

By E.S. Budd

The Child's World® Inc.

Published by The Child's World®, Inc.

Design and Production:
The Creative Spark, San Juan Capistrano, CA

Photos: © 1999 David M. Budd Photography

Library of Congress Cataloging-in-Publication Data

Budd, E.S.
       Street cleaners / by E.S. Budd.
            p. cm.
       Summary: Simple text describes street cleaning machines, what they do and how they work.
       ISBN 1-56766-757-0 (lib. bdg.)
       1. Street cleaning—Equipment and supplies—Juvenile literature. [1. Street cleaning—
Equipment and supplies.] I. Title.

    TD860 .B77 2000
    628.4'6--dc21
                                                            99-089471

Contents

On the Job

On the job, street cleaners keep our neighborhoods clean. City streets can get very dirty! Street cleaners drive next to a **curb.**

6

A street cleaner has many mirrors.

They help the driver see all around.

They also help the driver make sure

the street cleaner is working correctly.

A street cleaner has three big **brushes.** There are two side brushes. One is on the left side of the street cleaner. The other is on the right side. These brushes sweep the side of the road. They move dirt under the street cleaner.

Now the rear brush has a job to do.

It picks up the dirt the other

brushes left behind. All the dirt

goes into a **bin.**

Now the bin is full. It is time to throw

the dirt away. Up, up, up goes the bin.

The street cleaner dumps the dirt into a big pile at the city dump. Now it is ready to clean another street!

Climb Aboard!

Would you like to see where the driver sits? The driver has two steering wheels. He uses the left steering wheel when he uses the left side brush. He uses the right steering wheel when he uses the right side brush. The street cleaner has **controls** that help the driver run it.

Up Close

The inside

1. The steering wheels
2. The controls
3. The driver's seat

The outside

1. The bin

2. The nozzle

3. The side brush

4. The rear brush

5. The water tank

Glossary

bin (BIN)
A bin is a box on top of a street cleaner. Dirt is stored inside the bin.

brushes (BRUH-shez)
Brushes are tools that are used for sweeping or scrubbing. A street cleaner has three brushes.

controls (kun-TROLZ)
Controls are tools that are used to help make something work. A driver uses controls to make a street cleaner work.

curb (KERB)
A curb is a raised edge between a street and a sidewalk. Street cleaners drive next to curbs.

fire hydrant (FY-er HY-drent)
A fire hydrant is a pipe attached to a city's water supply. A fire hydrant is used to fill a street cleaner's water tank.

nozzle (NAH-zull)
A nozzle is a tip that is attached to a tank or hose. A street cleaner's nozzle sprays water on the street.

tank (TANGK)
A tank is a large container that holds liquids. A street cleaner has a water tank.